MW01516461

Away
in a
Manger

DAILY PRAYERS
FOR *Advent* AND *Christmas* 2025

WRITTEN BY JOSH NOEM

AVE MARIA PRESS AVE Notre Dame, Indiana

Scripture texts in this work are taken from the *New American Bible, revised edition* © 2010, 1991, 1986, 1970 Confraternity of Christian Doctrine, Washington, DC, and are used by permission of the copyright owner. All Rights Reserved. No part of the *New American Bible* may be reproduced in any form without permission in writing from the copyright owner.

Nihil Obstat: Reverend Monsignor Michael Heintz, PhD
             Censor Librorum

Imprimatur: Most Reverend Kevin C. Rhoades
           Bishop of Fort Wayne–South Bend
           Given at Fort Wayne, Indiana, on April 22, 2025

Writer
Josh Noem

© 2025 by Ave Maria Press, Inc.

All rights reserved. No part of this book may be used or reproduced in any manner whatsoever, except in the case of reprints in the context of reviews, without written permission from Ave Maria Press®, Inc., P.O. Box 428, Notre Dame, IN 46556, 1-800-282-1865.

Founded in 1865, Ave Maria Press is a ministry of the United States Province of Holy Cross.

www.avemariapress.com

Paperback: ISBN-13 978-1-64680-419-1

E-book: ISBN-13 978-1-64680-420-7

Cover image © *Angels Rejoicing* by FaithArtCreation (faithartcreation.etsy.com). Used with permission.

Cover design by Samantha Watson.

Text design by Katherine Robinson.

Printed and bound in the United States of America.

Introduction

The word *devotion* has its roots in the Latin word for *vow*, so the different shapes this word takes—*devoted* or *devout*, for example—communicate some kind of commitment and loyalty. A devotional simply takes that faithfulness and makes it accessible through a religious practice. It's a four-syllable word that points to everyday, practical steps we take to grow closer to God in love.

If you're not sure how to go about deepening your relationship with God, you're in the right book! This devotional offers brief prompts for reflection and prayer to assist you each day from November 30, the first Sunday of Advent this year, through January 11, the Feast of the Baptism of the Lord. This season of remembering and celebrating the Nativity of Christ is the perfect time to anchor ourselves in God's abiding presence.

The title for this devotional—*Away in a Manger*—comes from a well-known Christmas hymn, and the first word in that song reminds us how the Lord of heaven and earth came to us. He did not arrive in worldly glory, nor in the comforts of security—he came to us *away*, while his parents were traveling and had sought shelter in a corner of a barn outside a small, no-nothing town. It's almost as if he found the most insignificant and exasperating conditions possible just to prove that nowhere is too far away for him to meet us there. The devotions of this book will help you welcome him with music, brief reflections, and most especially prayer.

We will pray together in this booklet in a very Catholic way: with music. You've never seen a Catholic procession without a hymn for a reason—prayerful songs involve our whole bodies. Music engages our emotions: We use it to "lift up our hearts," as we say at Mass. Each day of this devotional opens with a lyric from a well-known Advent or Christmas hymn. A short reflection on that text follows, along with prayers for morning and evening and a simple spiritually focused question to think about throughout your day.

To help you pray, you can access a playlist of the songs featured in this book at www.avemariapress.com/pages/away-in-a-manger-music via your web browser or the QR codes that appear throughout this book (just focus

1

your smartphone's camera on the box code, and it will surface a link to this page). Each song used here has multiple versions available for you to linger over and pray with as you listen. You can find the complete lyrics for each song beginning on page 46.

Christ isn't waiting for Christmas to arrive in our hearts. Christ is with us now—in silence and song, wonder and joy—ready to enfold us in a loving embrace. Let us go to meet him together!

Ave Maria Press is a publishing ministry of the Congregation of Holy Cross, a religious order with a mission to educate in the faith by forming minds and hearts and drawing people into community. This book draws on the spirit that animates these priests and brothers—especially their devotion to the Holy Family, whose hopes and joys we enter during this season. The Press was founded more than 150 years ago to honor Mary, support the spiritual needs of our everyday living, and showcase the best American Catholic writing.

Drawing on our Holy Cross heritage, Ave aims to set hearts on fire—and that's the aim and hope for this Advent and Christmas devotional. Thank you for being part of our family of faith!

Sunday, November 30

FIRST WEEK OF ADVENT

Marvel now, O heav'n and earth, that the Lord chose such a birth.

We begin our Advent by remembering that God moves toward us first. As much as we want to begin this season with a concerted effort to make room in our lives for Christ, we acknowledge that even this desire is a response to his presence stirring in our hearts.

Jesus is everything God wants to say to us, and through his birth, he tells us that *God comes to us*. Even in this moment as you read these words, God is reaching for you. You are here on this page with other believers because God sent his only Son for you in order to draw you near. The Lord of heaven and earth chose to enter our humanity as a trembling baby in Bethlehem, and he is here with us now as we begin this Advent journey together.

Prayer for the Morning

Lord Jesus, you came to reveal the fullness of God's love. As I begin this Advent, increase my awareness of your presence, for you are already here with me, drawing me to yourself. Jesus, Our Brother, be near me today.

Ponder for the Day

As I ponder the birth of Jesus, how might I draw near and share life with someone today?

Prayer for the Evening

Lord Jesus, you make your home in our humanity not to rule over us but to reign within us. Grant me perseverance and attentiveness this Advent season that I might find my home in you. Jesus, Our Brother, I marvel at your love for me.

To listen to "Savior of the Nations Come," scan the QR code or visit www.avemariapress.com/pages/away-in-a-manger-music.

Monday, December 1

FIRST WEEK OF ADVENT

O wondrous Child . . . tho' by all the world disowned,
still to be in heav'n enthroned.

Not only does Jesus reveal that God comes to share life with us, but his appearance proves that God is willing to be rejected by humanity for the sake of love. God became human in Christ Jesus, knowing that he would be renounced by many. Such is the sign and wonder of God's love. And yet still he comes to us, relentlessly and passionately.

God knows that we are fallen and sinful and broken and imperfect, and these are the very reasons he came to live among us. God, in Jesus, reaches for us knowing our limitations, and in the mystery of his abundant and unending love, raises us up through them. What do we have to fear from him? What more could we ask?

Prayer for the Morning

Jesus, God-with-us, you give us all. Help me to step into your transformative love that I might reflect your presence to others today. Emmanuel, help me share your generosity.

Ponder for the Day

What are the habits through which you sometimes turn away from God's love? What can you do to change these?

Prayer for the Evening

Jesus, God-with-us, you pursue us despite our inadequacies. May my gratitude and wonder increase as I come to welcome your embrace. Emmanuel, enlarge my heart.

To listen to "Savior of the Nations Come," scan the QR code or visit

Tuesday, December 2

FIRST WEEK OF ADVENT

Boundless shall thy kingdom be; when shall we its glories see?

We know the world is not right—that we're meant for more. We are here, praying through Advent, because we want to see God's glory more fully. We yearn for God's reign in the world and in our own hearts.

The Church gives us this season of preparation to change our vision—to train our eyes and hearts to recognize the ways God's kingdom is breaking forth in our lives. Yes, the kingdom of God will break through in glory at the end of time, but it is also happening now. God is waiting to meet us in the small and ordinary moments of our lives—even the ones that unfold today—for nothing is beyond God's reign.

Prayer for the Morning

O God, Ruler of All, you created us with a driving desire to seek you and the order you bring to the world. Increase my desire for you and hone my attentiveness that I might recognize you when you appear in the circumstances of my life. Almighty One, I trust in you.

Ponder for the Day

What is one small way in which I can further God's kingdom in the unfolding of my day?

Prayer for the Evening

God, Ruler of All, your kingdom is boundless. Reach into the darkest and most hidden corners of my life, and bring me peace and rest with the light of your love. Almighty One, I long to see your glory.

www.avemariapress.com/pages/away-in-a-manger-music.

Wednesday, December 3

First Week of Advent

Keep your lamps trimmed and burning; the day is drawing nigh.

In the parable of the ten virgins (Mt 25:1–13), Jesus invites us to imagine a group of bridesmaids who take their lamps and go out to wait for the bridegroom's arrival. Five bring oil for their lamps; five do not. When the bridegroom finally arrives, those who did not prepare resources to welcome him miss the feast. "Therefore, stay awake," Jesus tells us, "for you know neither the day nor the hour."

The tradition of African American spirituals has taken this call to "keep your lamps trimmed and burning" and created a song to encourage endurance and hope. This is a steady march born from a people who know suffering, and who also know how to wait in that darkness with confidence that light is coming. Let's bring that same steady confidence to our Advent journey today.

Prayer for the Morning

Lord Jesus, you come to us like daylight scattering darkness. Preserve me in hope and grant me confidence that you will break into my life like the morning sun. Jesus, help me stay alert to your presence today.

Ponder for the Day

How can I bring intentionality and preparation to my spiritual life so that my lamp stays trimmed and burning?

Prayer for the Evening

Lord Jesus, you come to bring us into the feast of God's kingdom. My heart is burning to welcome you into my life. Through my prayer, draw me closer to you. Jesus, Our Bridegroom, I wait for you.

To listen to "Keep Your Lamps Trimmed and Burning," scan the QR

Thursday, December 4

FIRST WEEK OF ADVENT

Children, don't get weary till your work is done.

We are only at the very start of our Advent journey and have a long way to go. There is much to do between now and Christmas, and we don't want to neglect what's most important: preparing to celebrate Jesus as God's love made flesh.

It is easy to get weary with all the extra tasks of this season that stack on top of daily life. Many of us are also carrying grief or wrestling with despair, and these burdens get magnified when the world tells us we should be feeling joy and holiday cheer.

Yet here we are, showing up to reflect and pray together with a song that is sturdy enough to have carried generations of people through hardship to hope. We may feel tired, but we're not weary, because Jesus promised to be with us in our togetherness.

Prayer for the Morning

God Our Father, you do not leave us to carry our burdens alone. Help me be faithful to the work I have today, and may the faith that you are with me keep me from growing weary. Heavenly Father, give me strength.

Ponder for the Day

Who else in my life might be carrying a burden in this season—and how might we walk together?

Prayer for the Evening

God Our Father, you sent your Son to walk with us through every darkness and bring us into life. Grant me perseverance and a steady heart that I might be faithful to my Advent preparation—and bring me true joy in our Christmas feast. Heavenly Father, give me hope.

code or visit www.avemariapress.com/pages/away-in-a-manger-music.

Friday, December 5

FIRST WEEK OF ADVENT

Watchman, tell us of the night, what its signs of promise are.

This song takes the form of a dialogue between a watchman standing guard over a city and a traveler arriving after journeying through the night. The watchman has been on guard, and the traveler has been trekking through the dark. These are good shoes for us to fill in this Advent season—as both pilgrim and watcher, we are also looking for the light.

Like the traveler, we know what it's like to navigate through darkness, when our way is shadowed by grief, loneliness, despair, brokenness, and sinful habits that close us off from others. We look for insight from those who are watchful, who are attuned to the nuances of the landscape. Like pilgrims nearing their destination as dawn is about to break, we are urgently seeking signs of promise.

Prayer for the Morning

Jesus, Our Way, you are here with us, closer than we can imagine. Be with me as I walk through this day that I might follow your path of love. Morning Star, I look for your light.

Ponder for the Day

Who are the people in my life who are watchful and attentive to the way the Lord moves in their life—and what can I learn from their example?

Prayer for the Evening

Jesus, Our Way, you came to travel through the human condition with us—to share life with us in every way, even unto death. Grant me urgency in my search for your promise of life and light. Morning Star, guide me.

To listen to "Watchman, Tell Us of the Night," scan the QR code or

Saturday, December 6

FIRST WEEK OF ADVENT

Traveler, what a wondrous sight: see that glory-beaming star.

We rejoin the dialogue of this hymn today, this time from the position of the watchman standing atop an outlook as a traveler approaches and asks for news of what we've seen. If we've been attentive to God's movement through this first week of Advent, we've noticed his presence with us. The next step in our Advent journey is to relay to others the hope that this encounter brings.

We do not need to provide light to those who are journeying through darkness—we just need to point them to the light that is dawning on us. The dispositions we need to answer this call are perfect for our Advent practice: vigilance and stillness that come from being centered in God.

Prayer for the Morning

Jesus Christ, you are the light of the world. May my encounter with you in this moment make me ready to recognize and respond to the needs of the people you will put in my life today. Light of My Life, make me ready to proclaim your good news.

Ponder for the Day

Who will approach me today in need of light and hope? How can I be ready to respond?

Prayer for the Evening

Jesus Christ, you are the Father's embrace of our humanity. As I look for your presence, meet me in this moment of stillness. Light of My Life, reveal your love to me.

visit www.avemariapress.com/pages/away-in-a-manger-music.

Sunday, December 7

SECOND WEEK OF ADVENT

It came, a flower bright, amid the cold of winter
when half-gone was the night.

This hymn compares Christ to an ever-blooming rose that brings fragrant beauty to our lives. Notice how the song depicts Christ arriving in inhospitable conditions—like a rose arriving in the cold and dark of winter. For those of us who live in the northern climate, it would be shocking to see a brightly colored rose blooming in the cold at a time when nothing is growing and everything is gray.

But lo! This is the mysterious revelation of divine love that we are preparing to celebrate at Christmas. Behold Christ springing from the tender shoot of God's mercy—even here and now as you read this today. He comes to each of us unexpectedly, undeservedly—and he arrives with beauty to brighten even the cold and gray pieces of our lives.

Prayer for the Morning

Jesus, Our Rose, you carry to us the beauty of the Father's love. Help me to recognize and be grateful for the surprising ways you will break into my life today. Beautiful One, bloom in my life today.

Ponder for the Day

Where would you least expect to find God's presence speaking to you today? How can you be ready to recognize his beauty?

Prayer for the Evening

Jesus, Our Rose, you bloom eternal as the answer to our longing. Bring color and life to the places of my life where I feel cold and dreary. Beautiful One, I look for your tenderness.

To listen to "Lo, How a Rose E'er Blooming," scan the QR code or visit

Monday, December 8

Solemnity of the Immaculate Conception

Isaiah 'twas foretold it, the Rose I have in mind:
with Mary we behold it, the virgin mother kind.

Mary was the first to encounter Jesus as God's Word-made-flesh when he began to take shape in her womb. She leads us on our journey through Advent as we increase our capacity to behold him growing, taking shape, in our own lives.

Today's feast reminds us that Mary was born sinless so that she could more perfectly receive this Word. She is our "virgin mother kind," and we follow her purity and single-heartedness so that we can also encounter this Word—and, with her, learn to speak it boldly to the world.

Prayer for the Morning

Mary, Our Mother, you were blessed with God's grace in order to receive and bear Jesus to us. Pray for me that grace might transform me this Advent to better receive and bear Jesus to others. Virgin Mother, lead me to deeper holiness.

Ponder for the Day

What habits or unhealthy attachments distract me from what God wants to do with my life?

Prayer for the Evening

Mary, Our Mother, you knew how to hear God speaking in your life. Help me listen for God's Word and, like you, trust his promises. Virgin Mother, lead me to your son.

www.avemariapress.com/pages/away-in-a-manger-music.

Tuesday, December 9

SECOND WEEK OF ADVENT

*This Flower, whose fragrance tender with sweetness fills the air,
dispels with glorious splendor the darkness everywhere.*

As Christians, we believe Jesus saves us—he came among us to live and die and open to us a way to heaven. We celebrate what he has done for us as a people, but Jesus also came to save each one of us, personally and individually, intimately and with unending passion. His love is the only thing strong enough to pull us out of brokenness and sin. His love is the only thing in this life that won't disappoint us or fall away.

Note how this song describes the way Jesus, the Rose, triumphs—he comes into our darkness and fills it with sweet fragrance. He comes to inhabit our darkness with us—and, by sharing it, he transforms it into a place of beauty.

Prayer for the Morning

Jesus, Our Sweetness, you are always ready to break into our lives with the fragrance of divine love. Dispel the darkness that creeps into my life with your tenderness and truth. Emmanuel, Our Hope and Peace, carry me today.

Ponder for the Day

What is the darkest part of my life—and how can I invite Jesus to meet me there?

Prayer for the Evening

Jesus, Our Sweetness, you came to bring freedom to the captive and sight to the blind. Come into my life with your power to heal. Emmanuel, Our Hope and Peace, make me whole.

To listen to "Lo, How a Rose E'er Blooming," scan the QR code or visit

Wednesday, December 10

SECOND WEEK OF ADVENT

True man, yet very God,
from sin and death he saves us and lightens every load.

We celebrate Jesus's birth as one of our greatest feasts because it means God is with us, even here and even now. No matter if we've fallen or if we are faithful, we are God's beloved, and nothing can take that dignity away. Though we step into sin over and over, God's love means we don't have to measure ourselves by the worst things we've done. We are the Father's children, and Christ is our brother.

This undeserved love is offered without reservation. It's up to us to welcome it, which is to say, it is up to us to welcome *him*—Jesus who is true man and true God. He didn't come to remove the burden of life from us—we still face suffering and death, after all—but he comes to lighten our load by carrying it alongside us.

Prayer for the Morning

God, Our Father, your love for us knows no bounds. Help me to open my life to your Son, Jesus, so that, through his friendship, I might fall deeper in love with you. Rock of Our Salvation, hold me close today.

Ponder for the Day

What is one task or situation I'm facing today that might be easier to bear if I invite Jesus to face it with me?

Prayer for the Evening

God, Our Father, you pursue us to the ends of the earth. Deepen my trust in you and help me to do your will, for this is the only way I'll find joy and life. Rock of Our Salvation, I cling to you.

www.avemariapress.com/pages/away-in-a-manger-music.

Thursday, December 11

SECOND WEEK OF ADVENT

*Buenos días, paloma blanca, hoy te vengo a saludar,
saludando a tu belleza en tu trono celestial.*

Good morning, White Dove, today I come to greet you,
saluting your beauty on your heavenly throne.

Catholics in this country have been cooking for days and practicing music for weeks—all for a feast that celebrates the appearance of Mary to St. Juan Diego in 1531.

For us Catholics of the Americas, the Virgencita Morena is uniquely *ours*—she is Our Lady of Guadalupe, who came to us on our continent. What better time to recall this miracle than during Advent as we contemplate that not only did God send his Son to us as a child, but he sent his own mother to us as well. So we make preparations to celebrate this feast as robustly as we can: with music, food, dance, bright costumes, and flowers. And we sing this midnight serenade to Our Lady.

Prayer for the Morning

Mother of the Creator, you come to meet us where we are to proclaim the good news of God's saving love. Help me grow in anticipation for your son's coming today. White Dove, pray that I might deepen my faith.

Ponder for the Day

How can I practice Our Lady's purity and simplicity today?

Prayer for the Evening

Mother of the Creator, tonight, we praise your sweet name. I give you thanks for your care for us. White Dove, give me your blessing.

To listen to "Mañanitas Guadalupanas," scan the QR code or visit

Friday, December 12

FEAST OF OUR LADY OF GUADALUPE

Qué linda está la mañana, el aroma de las flores.
Despiden suaves olores antes de romper el alba.

How beautiful is the morning, the scent of the flowers.
They give off soft fragrance before the dawn breaks.

St. Juan Diego was an Aztec convert to Catholicism, and Our Lady spoke to him in the language of his native culture; she appeared as a *mestiza*, a woman with mixed European and indigenous features. In Aztec tradition, encounters with the divine were marked with music and flowers—and those are the signs with which Mary appeared to Juan Diego.

As her children, we use those same signs to give her honor. We offer her roses and music because we recognize her spiritual (and physical) beauty as the one who bears Jesus to us. By creating and enjoying beauty, we get a glimpse into God's dreams for us—and they are fragrant, bright, and sweet.

Prayer for the Morning

La Virgen, on this blessed day, we recall your coming to Juan Diego and the people of the Americas. Help me recognize the ways in which God is breaking into my life today. Our Lady, enchant me with beauty.

Ponder for the Day

Today, how can I notice and appreciate small moments of beauty as an expression of God's love for me?

Prayer for the Evening

La Virgen, we greet you today and sing to your beauty. Help me embrace your trusting vulnerability and so step into the dreams God has for my life. Our Lady, receive my humble heart.

www.avemariapress.com/pages/away-in-a-manger-music.

Saturday, December 13

SECOND WEEK OF ADVENT

Madre mía de Guadalupe, dame ya tu bendición.
My mother of Guadalupe, give me now your blessing.

This second week of Advent placed us at the feet of Mary, the Immaculate Conception and Our Lady of Guadalupe. Generations have approached and venerated Mary under these grand titles, but they can sometimes create a distance between us and our heavenly mother. It's not always easy to remember what she said to Juan Diego when he was nervous about all the uncertainty he was facing: "Do not let your heart be troubled. . . . Am I not here, I who am your Mother?"

Mary under any title is our Mother of Grace—she's a person who cares for each one of us with a fierce maternal love. When we approach her with loving familiarity, she will respond. She wants nothing more than to hold us close and bring us to her son, where we will find truth, peace, and joy.

Prayer for the Morning

Our Lady, you approach us with loving tenderness and invite us to draw on your help. Protect me and lead me to greater faith, hope, and love. Mother Mary, be near me today.

Ponder for the Day

How can I approach Mary with childlike humility and wonder today to ask for her help on my Advent journey?

Prayer for the Evening

Our Lady, you were the first to move through Advent when you bore the child Jesus. Help me grow in patient perseverance, especially when my way is unclear and confusing. Mother Mary, pray for me.

To listen to "Mañanitas Guadalupanas" or "On Jordan's Bank the

Sunday, December 14

THIRD WEEK OF ADVENT

On Jordan's bank the Baptist's cry announces that the Lord is nigh.

John the Baptist sits at the crossroads of the Old Testament and New Testament—the last of the great prophets and the first to recognize Jesus as the Messiah—the Lamb of God. He's a compelling Advent figure for us because we, too, are seeking to recognize the coming of Our Lord. What can we learn from John in our Advent searching?

The song we pray with today reminds us that John made his proclamation from the bank of the River Jordan, which runs through the dry and barren wilderness. He spent most of his time in solitude and silence, which gave him room to cultivate his interior life with God. That relationship gave John the vision to see what others couldn't—that in Jesus, God ushered in a new relationship with all of creation, one established in communion.

Prayer for the Morning

God of Silence, you spoke to John when he was alone with his thoughts in the wilderness. Help me embrace moments of quiet today as opportunities to listen for your voice. God of Stillness, draw ever near.

Ponder for the Day

What habits prevent me from cultivating a rich interior life where I can recognize and attend to God's presence?

Prayer for the Evening

God of Silence, you empowered John to recognize and proclaim the coming of your Son. Grant me the vision to see Christ present in my life and to share his love with others. God of Stillness, help me announce your nearness.

Baptist's Cry," scan the QR code or visit www.avemariapress.com/pages/away-in-a-manger-music.

Monday, December 15

Third Week of Advent

Awake and harken, for he brings
glad tidings of the King of kings!

This lyric reminds us of the great summons of Advent to wake up and listen. This season is a time to recognize the ways in which we are not fully awake, not tuned into Christ's presence. We know there are parts of our lives that need to change for us to live with deeper faithfulness. The conversion we seek begins with the listening we are doing in prayer, because Christ is already here, leading us as he remains by our side.

Especially in this holiday season, when there are so many demands on our attention and desires, our challenge is to pay attention to the ways Christ is speaking to us, especially through the people in our lives who carry glad tidings of his kingdom.

Prayer for the Morning

Lord Jesus, as God's Incarnate Word, you speak to us in the circumstances of our lives. Deepen my patience and generosity today that I might recognize your presence with me in the here and now, no matter what this day brings. King of Kings, I listen for your voice.

Ponder for the Day

Where might I listen and watch today for glad tidings of God's kingdom?

Prayer for the Evening

Lord Jesus, you come to us with the intent to rule our lives with love. Stir my heart and imagination that I might recognize your faithful care for me and have courage to trust in your providence. King of Kings, I look for your guidance.

To listen to "On Jordan's Bank the Baptist's Cry," scan the QR code

Tuesday, December 16

THIRD WEEK OF ADVENT

Then cleansed be every life from sin: make straight the way for God within, and let us all our hearts prepare for Christ to come and enter there.

We all have created crooked ways inside our hearts—we bend the truth to suit our egos, we scheme to get our own way, and we look down on others in order to feel superior. We are praying through this Advent season together so that we can stop traveling along these crooked ways and instead clear a path on which we can meet and walk with God.

This is a journey we make together—it helps to be part of a people moving in the same direction, week by week. The more we sense his nearness, the more urgency we feel. We don't want to wander or waste time—we want to walk straight toward him with direction and purpose.

Prayer for the Morning

God, Our Hope, you send your Son to enter and dwell within each of us. Grant me courage to see with clarity the ways I've made your way crooked, and help me straighten my heart to yearn for you alone. God, Our Joy, cleanse me from sin.

Ponder for the Day

What are the crooked ways of my heart that I need to straighten in order to encounter God more directly?

Prayer for the Evening

God, Our Hope, your Son clears a way for your Spirit to bring us into union with you. Meet me in my efforts to prepare room for your love in my life. God, Our Joy, come and enter.

or visit www.avemariapress.com/pages/away-in-a-manger-music.

Wednesday, December 17

THIRD WEEK OF ADVENT

Comfort, comfort ye my people, speak ye peace, thus saith our God.
Comfort those who sit in darkness, mourning neath
their sorrows' load.

This song draws on the words of the prophet Isaiah, who heard God calling him to proclaim comfort to his people who lived in the despair of exile. Isaiah's writing offered hope for those in darkness, and it has been cherished and passed down to us because we, too, live in exile. We are separated from one another because of our brokenness; we are distanced from ourselves because of our competing desires.

But God's promises of comfort are fulfilled in Christ. He comes to bear our load of sorrow with us—and in sharing our suffering, he transforms it into a life-giving path to union with God. This is the good news of comfort and joy that we, too, are called to proclaim by the ways we choose to live.

Prayer for the Morning

Jesus, Word of Life, you echo through the ages as God's comfort to his people. Help me remember that my Advent preparations are not a passive waiting but an active participation in the ways you are already here with us. Christ, Our Peace, help me announce the hope you bring.

Ponder for the Day

Who is someone in my life who sits beneath a load of sorrow? How can I show that person a sign of God's promise of comfort?

Prayer for the Evening

Jesus, Word of Life, you speak God's peace to us. As the darkness of this night wears on, I sit with you. Christ, Our Peace, bring me your light.

To listen to "Comfort, Comfort Ye My People," scan the QR code or

Thursday, December 18

Third Week of Advent

Make ye straight what long was crooked,
make the rougher places plain;
let your hearts be true and humble, as befits his holy reign.

Because we are using Advent as a time to recognize God's nearness, we must also attend to the state of our interior life, for this is the place where we find God's holy reign within ourselves. We cannot have disorder in our hearts if we want to meet there the author of order—the One who put into motion all things, from the stars in the heavens to the stirrings of our own hearts.

So, we are about the work of making the rough places of our lives smooth and plain. In order to welcome God's reign, we must first know and live by who we really are: his beloved children. This acknowledgment requires the humility to let go of any other markers on which we stake our lives and to put our lives in the hands of our loving Father.

Prayer for the Morning

Heavenly Father, you seek us out with relentless love. Widen my heart to welcome your reign, and help me to live as your beloved child. Author of Life, make my heart true.

Ponder for the Day

What gets in the way of God's reign in me? What rough parts of my heart do I need to smooth?

Prayer for the Evening

Heavenly Father, you are holy and created us for union with you. Make me holy by burning away the things that pull my heart away from you. Author of Life, make my heart humble.

visit www.avemariapress.com/pages/away-in-a-manger-music.

Friday, December 19

THIRD WEEK OF ADVENT

Wake, awake, for night is flying,
the watchmen on the heights are crying; . . .
"Come forth, you maidens! Night is past.
The Bridegroom comes! Awake!"

We are less than a week away from our Christmas feast. This season has been flying along like the waning hours of the night, but it is not too late to prepare ourselves to meet the Lord.

In the midst of our end-of-the-year projects and holiday tasks and family obligations, attending to our Advent prayerfulness is a challenge. The week ahead will be filled with urgency and anticipation, but the kind of attentiveness we really need this season is found in stillness. The Lord's presence arrives with small signs that are easy to miss, but those who are watching will recognize him.

Prayer for the Morning

Christ, Our Bridegroom, you are God's expression of love for us. With all the concerns and questions and reminders clamoring for my attention today, meet me in my prayer. Dayspring, bring your light.

Ponder for the Day

How can I preserve an attentive watchfulness throughout my day today?

Prayer for the Evening

Christ, Our Bridegroom, your light stirs those who wait for the dawn of your love. Intensify my urgency and anticipation for the ways you break into my life. Dayspring, remain with me.

To listen to "Wake, Awake, for Night Is Flying," scan the QR code or

Saturday, December 20

THIRD WEEK OF ADVENT

She wakes, she rises from her gloom,
for her Lord comes down all-glorious,
and strong in grace, in truth victorious.
Her star is ris'n; her light is come.

Though he is Creator of heaven and earth, God did not set the universe into motion and step away. Rather, he stepped *into* it himself. In sending his Son to share life with us, the Father does not remain distant and aloof. He "comes down all-glorious" to share life with us. We don't need to leave the details of our experience behind to seek him, for in Christ, God is found by going *deeper into* the circumstances of our lives.

Our Father knows what causes us fear and shame and despair—he knows our darkness better than we do. He comes to each of us with grace and truth to conquer our gloom, but only if we let him in. Our light is come—it is time to ready ourselves for the new day it brings.

Prayer for the Morning

Faithful One, there is nowhere we can go to escape your concern and affection. Be patient with me as I come to more deeply trust that you are all I need. Everlasting Light, bring your strong grace.

Ponder for the Day

What is a source of gloom in my life—and how is God leading me to awaken from it?

Prayer for the Evening

Faithful One, you know and love us with reckless abandon. Sharpen my vision for the things that hold me back from living more fully in the love you so freely give. Everlasting Light, bring your victorious truth.

visit www.avemariapress.com/pages/away-in-a-manger-music.

Sunday, December 21

FOURTH WEEK OF ADVENT

Make your house fair as you are able, trim the hearth and set the table.
People, look east and sing today: Love, the guest, is on the way.

Final preparations are abuzz right now with gifts to find, packages to mail, pantries to stock. "People, Look East" is a good song to bring merriment and joy to those tasks—the melody can keep us on our toes and brighten our disposition while we're waiting in line and swimming through crowds.

Let's recall the most important reason we are busy: We are preparing for the arrival anew of one who humbled himself to be with us in our humanity and to bring us undeserved gifts of the Father's unconditional love. The arrival of Jesus is cause for great rejoicing, and we gather with friends and family to celebrate together. So we sing our way through our to-do list today, for Love, the guest, is on the way.

Prayer for the Morning

Lord of Love, you are the unreserved self-gift of the Father, and you come to bring us into fullness of life. Brighten my gratitude and joy as I prepare to celebrate your arrival. Jesus, Our Guest, ready your way in me.

Ponder for the Day

What part of my life feels distant from God right now? How might I recognize Christ approaching me there?

Prayer for the Evening

Lord of Love, you draw close to us even when we are unfaithful and feel distant from God. Make me know your nearness that I might find joy and purpose. Jesus, Our Guest, I welcome you into my life.

To listen to "People, Look East," scan the QR code or visit

Monday, December 22

FOURTH WEEK OF ADVENT

Furrows, be glad. Though earth is bare,
one more seed is planted there:
give up your strength the seed to nourish,
that in course the flower may flourish.

Here in the Northern Hemisphere, we are aware of shorter amounts of daylight as we draw near the winter solstice. While we know the sunlight will grow through the spring, we are still a long way from that warmth. We can take a lesson from the barren earth in this season when important things are happening below the surface. This is a time to attend to what is quiet and hidden, to nourish buried roots. God will give us what we need to grow. With patience and trust, we will flourish in his love.

Prayer for the Morning

Source of Life, you provide for our every need. Help me let go of the stubborn desire to obtain and control what I seem to think I need to flourish. Help me instead cling to you with confidence that you will care for me. Source of Love, I trust you.

Ponder for the Day

Where in your life is God asking you to be more patient and trusting?

Prayer for the Evening

Source of Life, you nourish us in order to make us more capable of growing closer to you. Let me not overlook your action in my life—help me to receive the gifts you offer. Source of Love, strengthen me.

www.avemariapress.com/pages/away-in-a-manger-music.

Tuesday, December 23

FOURTH WEEK OF ADVENT

Of her, Immanuel, the Christ, was born
in Bethlehem, all on a Christmas morn . . . Gloria[1]

No one in first-century Palestine would have associated Bethlehem with glory. Bethlehem was a small village everyone passed through on their way to Jerusalem, where glory abounded. If God was interested in our idea of glory, his Son would have been born six miles to the north.

God's glory shines in unexpected places. Consider the story of Mary and Joseph. God's revelation comes to them in small, hidden ways that had glorious consequences—a surprise pregnancy, a dream, childbirth on a night when they had no place to sleep. Jesus comes to us in the same way today. We cannot foresee the glory he has in store for us, but we know he is waiting for us in the quiet corners of our prayer. Our job is to meet him there and adore.

Prayer for the Morning

Mary, Full of Grace, God's Word came to you in a quiet, hidden moment of prayer. Help me greet your son in my prayer today and carry him as you did. Mary, Our Mother, bring me to your son.

Ponder for the Day

What are the hidden ways God might speak into your life today?

Prayer for the Evening

Mary, Full of Grace, you trusted in God's glory, even when the circumstances of your life looked grim and gloomy. Deepen my trust and increase my faith that I might see God at work in my life too. Mary, Our Mother, prepare me for glory.

To listen to "The Angel Gabriel from Heaven Came," scan the QR

Wednesday, December 24

Christmas Eve

Then gentle Mary meekly bowed her head;
"To me be as it pleases God," she said.
"My soul shall laud and magnify his holy name."

The angel Gabriel greeted Mary by naming her "most highly favored," yet Mary did not grasp at status. Her response to Gabriel was to redirect praise to God, for her whole life magnified the Lord. The key to Mary's faithfulness is humility, which is to know our place as creatures and God's place as Creator and then to conform our lives to his will. As our Advent preparations reach their fulfillment with the Christmas feast that begins this evening, we bow our heads with Mary and receive with wonder and gratitude the gifts God offers us.

Prayer for the Morning

Mary, Mother of God, your obedience opened the gates of heaven to us by bringing us our Savior. Help me more deeply embrace humility that I might grow confident in my reliance upon God. Mary, Mother of the Church, with you I magnify our God.

Ponder for the Day

What has been the greatest gift God has given you this Advent?

Prayer for the Evening

Mary, Mother of God, you had clarity about what was most important in this life, which gave you courage and direction even when the way was not clear. As I step into the Feast of the Nativity of your son, help me remember what is of eternal significance in this life. Mary, Mother of the Church, pray for me this Christmas season.

code or visit www.avemariapress.com/pages/away-in-a-manger-music.

Thursday, December 25

CHRISTMAS DAY

Angels we have heard on high, sweetly singing o'er the plains;
and the mountains in reply echoing their joyous strains.

The shepherds outside of Bethlehem on the night of Jesus's birth would have been familiar with the night sky and the quiet hills. They would have observed the noise and commotion and lights of the town die down as people settled in for the night. It's a peaceful scene, conducive to contemplation, with the blue light of the moon laying shadows across the fields, the only sound a light breeze punctuated by the munching and bleating of the sheep. We can imagine a sudden blast of light and song; the skies open, and angels appear hailing a new definitive chapter in salvation history: the birth of our Savior.

This good news comes to us today with no less grandeur and splendor—let us rejoice and proclaim it with joy!

Prayer for the Morning

Mighty One, the gift of your Son was proclaimed by a choir of angels. Help me receive the gift of our Savior with the urgent wonder and awe the shepherds felt at this good news. Faithful One, sing your glory in me.

Ponder for the Day

What is one small way you can reflect the wondrous gift of a Savior to someone today?

Prayer for the Evening

Mighty One, the birth of Jesus was announced with song and light. Today, I join these strains of joy and give you thanks for coming to share life with me. Faithful One, echo your glory in me.

To listen to "Angels We Have Heard on High," scan the QR code or

Friday, December 26

CHRISTMAS WEEKDAY

Gloria in excelsis Deo!

Praise is what we're made for. When we praise God, the world is rightly ordered: God is at the center, and we bring all of creation into orbit around him with our thanksgiving and wonder at his providing and all-powerful love for us.

There has never been a more fitting moment in human history for praise to ring out than at the moment of Jesus's birth, when God restored us by becoming one of us. We had fallen out of orbit, so he left the center and rushed to the margins to save us. The only thing we can do to respond to the mystery of this great gift is to exalt in God's love and join our voices with the angels to ring out over the hills and plains, "Glory to God in the highest!"

Prayer for the Morning

Almighty God, you don't need our praise, but it is all we can offer you in response to your great love for us. Accept my thanks and wonder at the intimacy with which you know and love me. Everlasting Father, I praise you.

Ponder for the Day

What is one thing you can do today as an offering of praise?

Prayer for the Evening

Almighty God, you created us as your beloved children and pursue us even with your own Son, even to the grave. Grant me confidence in your abiding love for me and help me hold fast to you. Everlasting Father, I exalt you.

visit www.avemariapress.com/pages/away-in-a-manger-music.

Saturday, December 27

CHRISTMAS WEEKDAY

Shepherds, why this jubilee?

Heaven could not contain itself when Christ was born. The glory of this moment spilled out into the hillsides surrounding Bethlehem, and it is interesting to note the first people who received the announcement of this good news. Shepherds were smelly, strange, and nomadic. They would have been seen by the people of Bethlehem as outsiders. They were probably the poorest people who were nearest to the Holy Family at that moment. It's as if the angels wanted to announce the coming of our Savior as soon as possible to the people in need of it most.

This is who Jesus came for—he came for us, especially when we are smelly and untrustworthy. Let us respond as the shepherds did—by seeking him out to honor and worship him with joy and wonder.

Prayer for the Morning

Jesus, Son of the Most High, you come to inaugurate a kingdom of peace and justice. Embolden me to join your mission to proclaim liberty to the oppressed and the Good News to the poor by advancing your kingdom. Emmanuel, use me to bring your love to others.

Ponder for the Day

Who are the poorest people nearest to you? What good news can you share with them? How?

Prayer for the Evening

Jesus, Son of the Most High, you come to deliver us from sin and death. Reach for me when I feel unworthy of your love. Emmanuel, stay with me.

To listen to "Angels We Have Heard on High" or "Away in a Manger,"

Sunday, December 28

FEAST OF THE HOLY FAMILY

The little Lord Jesus asleep on the hay.

This sweet song is a lullaby that helps us imagine Jesus as a child—even as a childlike companion to us. That's what his birth made us: brothers and sisters to him, the Word made flesh. This hymn puts us in the stable with Mary and Joseph, gazing down at the infant. What does it say about God that this child is the way by which he became one of us? Jesus could have come to us in any number of ways, and every circumstance surrounding his birth was contingent, vulnerable, and uncertain—except for the love of this family.

With love at the center of our relationships, no matter our family structure, we can weather anything—just as the Holy Family did.

Prayer for the Morning

Jesus, Mary, and Joseph, though you faced adversity and uncertainty, you were committed to one another and were willing to sacrifice yourselves for the good of the family. Help me invest in loving relationships that mirror your selflessness. Holy Family, make me holy through the people you place in my life.

Ponder for the Day

Who in your life lacks a solid foundation of loving relationships at home, and how can you support them?

Prayer for the Evening

Jesus, Mary, and Joseph, you found all you needed with one another. Deepen my commitment to my loved ones, and help me find in them a reflection of your intimacy. Holy Family, hold me close.

scan the QR code or visit www.avemariapress.com/pages/away-in-a-manger-music.

Monday, December 29

CHRISTMAS WEEKDAY

Away in a manger, no crib for a bed.

The first line of this song captures the most important detail of Jesus's birth—he came to us outside of the comfort of a home. From the very start, he identifies himself most closely with those of us who are displaced, who are without a home (sometimes even when we are *at* home), who don't have a place to belong, who are uncomfortable, who depend on the generosity of others for what we need. Jesus is here for those of us who don't even have a place to rest. He is here with a unique mission to be with those of us who are *away.*

Prayer for the Morning

Jesus, Love of the Father, your coming to us means that no one is beyond God's concern and care. Grant me your consoling presence when I feel distanced from myself and others. Jesus, Our Companion, walk close to me when I need your embrace.

Ponder for the Day

Who among your loved ones is away from you right now—either physically or emotionally—and what might you do to draw near to them?

Prayer for the Evening

Jesus, Love of the Father, your coming expanded the bounds of who belongs and binds all of us into an everlasting family. Grow your presence within me that I might overflow with your love. Jesus, Our Companion, help me walk with others who need your embrace.

To listen to "Away in a Manger," scan the QR code or visit

Tuesday, December 30

Christmas Weekday

Be near me, Lord Jesus; I ask thee to stay
close by me forever, and love me, I pray.

As people of faith, we keep Jesus as a familiar figure at the center of our lives. We know he was a historical person who lived, taught, and died in first-century Israel. We believe him to be the second person of the Trinity, the Word made flesh, and the Risen Lord. With all of the different ways to understand and encounter Jesus, we can sometimes overlook him as a simple *person*—as a friend who is very close to us and involved in our lives right now.

This hymn resonates with children because it puts into words the simple way Jesus wants to relate to us. Unless we adopt a childlike immediacy in our friendship with Jesus, considering him as a historical or religious figure doesn't matter. He came into this world to be near each one of us, and it is up to us to respond to his invitation to love us forever.

Prayer for the Morning

Beloved Jesus, you came to draw us into friendship with God. Inspire me to reach for you with simple faith, knowing that you want to be close to me and share my concerns and dreams. Be near me, Lord Jesus.

Ponder for the Day

How can you invite Jesus into your life today with simple, childlike friendship?

Prayer for the Evening

Beloved Jesus, you are closer to each of us than we are to ourselves. Deepen my understanding of myself that I might invite you to bring your light into every corner of my life. Lord Jesus, I ask thee to stay close by me forever.

www.avemariapress.com/pages/away-in-a-manger-music.

Wednesday, December 31

CHRISTMAS WEEKDAY

Fit us for heaven, to live with thee there.

Here on the last day of our secular calendar, we look back to see all the joys, sorrows, and blessings that 2025 has brought us. It is a good moment to recollect the ways God has led us and what he has asked of us this past year.

Through it all, we trust that God's singular focus is to bring us into union with him. The Father sent the Son to "fit us for heaven" that we might live forever in love with him. If that's the divine pedagogy at work in our lives, we can shift our perspective on what transpires in our lives—success and suffering alike only matter insomuch as they help us practice that union with God in this life. This has been the goal of our Advent and Christmas prayer too—to cultivate intimacy with God through his Son in our day-to-day living so that we grow in our capacity to carry his presence through this life and be carried by his love into the next.

Prayer for the Morning

Everlasting Father, life with you is our eternal dwelling place. Increase my desire to live with you forever and to bring intentionality to the ways I participate today in the divine life you offer. God of All Grace, make me one with you.

Ponder for the Day

How has God been moving in your life this year to draw you closer?

Prayer for the Evening

Everlasting Father, you are our glory and strength. Stir me to turn to you when I am in need and weak that I might more deeply rely on you in every aspect of my life. God of All Grace, fit me for heaven.

To listen to "Away in a Manger" or "Holy Is His Name," scan the QR

Thursday, January 1

SOLEMNITY OF MARY, THE HOLY MOTHER OF GOD

And Mary said:
"My soul proclaims the greatness of the Lord;
my spirit rejoices in God my savior."

Mary's Magnificat is a song of praise that she proclaims when she visits Elizabeth, and it gives us a window into Mary's state of mind after Gabriel's annunciation. The way she relates to God in this hymn shows us something of how she understands the mystery she's now at the center of.

The first thing she reveals in this hymn is that she sees God as a savior. Even before Jesus was born and accomplished our salvation on the Cross, Mary sees God acting in her life and in the life of her people as a savior. That's who God is—he comes to save us and will stop at nothing to reach us and do great things for us.

Prayer for the Morning

Holy Mary, Mother of God, you had a clear vision of who God is and how he acts in our lives to bring us into his love. Pray for me that I might recognize and welcome God's saving action in my own life. Mary, Our Mother in Faith, I proclaim God's greatness with you.

Ponder for the Day

What is something you need saving from? How can you invite God to take action there?

Prayer for the Evening

Holy Mary, Mother of God, you accepted your central role in our salvation with trust in God's greatness. Deepen my humility that I might join you in proclaiming the good news of God's saving love. Mary, Our Mother in Faith, my spirit rejoices with you.

code or visit www.avemariapress.com/pages/away-in-a-manger-music.

Friday, January 2

CHRISTMAS WEEKDAY

"He has thrown down the rulers from their thrones
but lifted up the lowly."

Mary's relationship with God allowed her to see the world as it is ordered according to grace. With the eyes of faith, she sees a power structure that turns the things of this world upside down. Mary's song is a longing to put things aright according to a different kind of logic, one where the arrogant are dispersed and the lowly are lifted up.

How do we align ourselves with this new understanding of power? How do we draw on it and find strength there? One way is to follow Mary's example into lowliness. God's power was not an abstract idea to her; she depended on it for her life. Faith was not a hobby or something she did as a side interest. It was at the center of her life.

Prayer for the Morning

Mother of Mercy, you found strength in God's power, enabling you to do what seemed impossible. Pray for me that I might also see the world with the logic of God's kingdom and lift up the lowly. Mary, Full of Grace, lead me.

Ponder for the Day

How can you put yourself in relationship with a population or an individual whom our culture generally sees as among the lowly today?

Prayer for the Evening

Mother of Mercy, you had eyes to see God's might changing the world. Deepen my faith that I might participate in his reign. Mary, Full of Grace, help me have the courage to put my life in God's hands.

To listen to "Holy Is His Name," scan the QR code or visit

Saturday, January 3

CHRISTMAS WEEKDAY

"He has helped Israel his servant,
remembering his mercy,
according to his promise to our fathers,
to Abraham and to his descendants forever."

God remembers his promise of mercy. People of faith who came before us lived by this promise and handed on to us their underlying trust in it. We can lean on their strength and hope, knowing that they believed with their very lives that God was faithful. That belief can sustain us as well. The generations who have gone before us faced crises no less heartbreaking than ours, and if they found that God is unfailingly merciful, then we can too. There are precious few truths we can stake our lives on in this world, but the closest thing we might find to certainty in faith is the billions of Christians who have found strength and courage in God's faithfulness while enduring every harsh reality that life can throw at a person.

Prayer for the Morning

Faithful One, you led our ancestors in faith, from Abraham and Moses to the saints of the twentieth century. Hold me close within this family of hope and love, and help me live in a way that hands this faith on to others. Merciful Father, lead me.

Ponder for the Day

Who are the people, living or dead, who have handed on faith to you, and how might you express gratitude for this gift?

Prayer for the Evening

Faithful One, your love for us never fails. Magnify your love in me and bring me safely into eternal life with you. Merciful Father, guide me.

www.avemariapress.com/pages/away-in-a-manger-music.

Sunday, January 4

THE EPIPHANY OF THE LORD

Let all mortal flesh keep silence, and with fear and trembling stand . . .
for, with blessing in his hand Christ our God to earth descendeth.

The Magi who traveled from the East to visit the newborn Christ knew they were in the presence of a great mystery. They arrived with gifts, asking nothing but to adore. Today, we join the Magi and bow at the feet of Christ our God who descended to join us in mortal flesh. Our culture puts Christmas in a tidy box with a bow on December 25, but we know that we are celebrating an event that changes the very nature of reality for us, and so we keep celebrating. The Magi saw the cosmic significance of this event, and we join them in silent wonder.

Prayer for the Morning

Christ Our God, the Magi's search led them to discover you in humble circumstances. Meet me in my desire to encounter you, and accept the meager gifts I have to offer. King of Kings, I long to see you.

Ponder for the Day

How can you bow before the wonder of God becoming human in the Incarnation today?

Prayer for the Evening

Christ Our God, the Magi followed signs of your coming and traveled to find you. Sharpen my perception of the signs you share today, and help me journey beyond myself to embrace you wherever you appear to me. King of Kings, I seek for you.

To listen to "Let All Mortal Flesh Keep Silence," scan the QR code or

Monday, January 5

CHRISTMAS WEEKDAY

Lord of lords, in human vesture, in the body and the blood.
He will give to all the faithful his own self for heav'nly food.

We've been preparing for and celebrating the gift of Jesus as divine love come to join our human lives "in the body and the blood." But our Savior doesn't stop with simply walking with us "in human vesture."

Jesus's coming opens a way for us to find God not by needing to distance ourselves from the things of the created world but instead by immersing ourselves in all their particularities. The deeper we know ourselves, our circumstances, our fears and dreams, the more we find ourselves walking with Christ. Jesus did not come to us as a superhero—he entered our weakness and joined our flesh, then went even further to give up his very body to die on the Cross in order to save us. As if becoming one with us and dying for the sake of our salvation weren't enough, he redoubles the gift by sharing the fullness of his being with us in the Eucharistic sacrifice and our reception of his Body and Blood in Holy Communion.

Prayer for the Morning

Jesus, God-with-us, you come to each of us with the total gift of yourself. Fortify me to hand over to you my weakness, knowing that you are waiting to meet me there. Bread of Life, strengthen me today.

Ponder for the Day

How can you nourish other people with the gift of yourself today, and thereby participate in Christ's selfless love?

Prayer for the Evening

Jesus, God-with-us, you sustain us with your Body and Blood. Make me worthy of the divine life you came to share. Bread of Life, nourish me.

visit www.avemariapress.com/pages/away-in-a-manger-music.

Tuesday, January 6

Christmas Weekday

Yet in thy dark streets shineth the everlasting light;
the hopes and fears of all the years are met in thee tonight.

Do you ever wonder if your life is important or significant enough for the God of creation to be concerned with you? If so, just look at Bethlehem. It was a no-nothing, backwater small town that served as a rest stop outside a major city. Yet this was the place where everlasting light broke into our world, where Jesus came to meet the "hopes and fears of all the years."

The fact that the Light of the World first shone in the dark streets of Bethlehem proves to us that God can be found in no-nothing places everywhere. Wise men did not overlook humble Bethlehem in their search for Jesus, and we should not overlook our own humble hearts as places where he wants to meet our hopes and fears.

Prayer for the Morning

Emmanuel, you spent most of your life in obscurity, and you had a special place in your heart for those on the margins. Ignite in me the fire of your love that I might share your love with those who need you. Everlasting Light, shine in me today.

Ponder for the Day

What are your most deeply held hopes and fears? And what light do you want Jesus to shed on them today?

Prayer for the Evening

Emmanuel, you came to bring us into intimacy with the Father. Help me to remember that no corner of my heart is too small or insignificant for your love. Everlasting Light, illumine my life.

To listen to "O Little Town of Bethlehem," scan the QR code or visit

Wednesday, January 7

CHRISTMAS WEEKDAY

O holy Child of Bethlehem, descend to us, we pray;
cast out our sin and enter in; be born in us today.

Much of our world is already weeks past Christmas. Even New Year's Day is fading in our consciousness as we wade into 2026. As people of faith, however, we continue to enjoy this Christmas feast. Still, we know that the mystery of God's Son coming to us is not confined to a few weeks each winter, for Christ is always seeking to be born in us. He is always ready to cast out our sin and enter in and be born in us anew.

The prayer we've been cultivating this Advent and Christmas season has helped us welcome Christ into our lives in new ways, which is a fundamental call of the Christian life: to invite Jesus to abide with us. Our task as we close this formal Christmas feast is to carry that friendship into the rest of the year.

Prayer for the Morning

Holy One of Israel, you descend into our lives to raise us up to the Father. Meet me in my prayer and lift me up to union with the Trinity. Holy Child of Bethlehem, be born in me today.

Ponder for the Day

What has been a helpful practice for my prayer life these past few weeks, and what can I carry into 2026?

Prayer for the Evening

Holy One of Israel, you are never far from us and respond when we call. Grant me perseverance and commitment in my life of prayer that I might remain close to you through the year ahead. Holy Child of Bethlehem, enter in.

www.avemariapress.com/pages/away-in-a-manger-music.

Thursday, January 8

CHRISTMAS WEEKDAY

Peace on the earth, good will to all,
from heaven's all-gracious King.

This song was written in 1849 by a preacher in New England named Edmund Sears. The year prior had seen unrest throughout Europe and the conclusion of the Mexican-American War—these events laid heavy on Sears's mind. Then, as now, the world was not heeding the message of the angels who appeared at Christ's birth to proclaim peace.

We hear about and see seemingly endless news of war in many places. We know that beyond the headlines lie dreadful suffering and barely comprehensible evils committed by our fellow human beings. Still, we wait in "solemn stillness" to hear the angels sing their glorious songs, committed to the hope that peace will come one day.

Prayer for the Morning

Wonder-Counselor, you came to usher into this world God's kingdom. Sustain me in my longing for the fulfillment of his reign, and grant me courage to do what I can to advance peace in our world. Prince of Peace, expand and strengthen my hope.

Ponder for the Day

Where does the lack of peace in the world most trouble you? Bring the people suffering there to your prayer today.

Prayer for the Evening

Wonder-Counselor, your angels proclaimed your coming with songs of peace. Attune my ears to recognize this song in the small and ordinary ways you are present to me every day. Prince of Peace, expand my faith.

To listen to "It Came Upon the Midnight Clear," scan the QR code or

Friday, January 9

Christmas Weekday

And ye, beneath life's crushing load,
whose forms are bending low. . . .
O rest beside the weary road, and hear the angels sing!

The author of these lyrics, Edmund Sears, was struggling with depression when he wrote these words. It is a song of hope from someone who knows what it's like to "toil along the climbing way with painful steps and slow."

Despite "life's crushing load," Sears had a vision that broke through the midnight clouds of his life: "Look now!" he wrote, "for glad and golden hours come swiftly on the wing." He calls us to rest along the weary road to hear the angels sing—to recognize and hold on to their promise of peace, quiet though it may be.

Faith reveals to us that good news of a Savior has broken into our world—into the lives of each one of us—and the fullness of that promise will not be wasted.

Prayer for the Morning

Christ Our Savior, you came to share life's crushing load. Give me strength to lean on you as I carry my burdens. Christ Our Life, console me.

Ponder for the Day

When have you seen "glad and golden hours" this Advent and Christmas season? What grace did you find there?

Prayer for the Evening

Christ Our Savior, your good news is not just for the world at-large—it is meant for each one of us in the particularities of our lives. Help me to believe in you as the Word of Life, come to fulfill God's promises. Christ Our Life, reveal yourself to me.

visit www.avemariapress.com/pages/away-in-a-manger-music.

Saturday, January 10

CHRISTMAS WEEKDAY

Our God, heaven cannot hold him, nor earth sustain;
heaven and earth shall flee away when he comes to reign:
in the bleak midwinter a stable place sufficed,
the Lord God Almighty, Jesus Christ.

The sun cannot withhold light. A tree cannot withhold shade. And God cannot withhold love—it's who God is. And because pure love is unconditional and ever generous, heaven could not contain God. So divine life spilled into the world in the person of Jesus Christ, and it pours into the hearts of each of us through the gift of faith.

Even if we are facing a bleak midwinter in our lives with challenges and struggles that never seem to relent, Jesus Christ comes to us. A stable sufficed for his birth—he will enter and abide within our lowly, humble hearts.

Prayer for the Morning

Jesus, God's Love, you are pure self-gift. Lead me your way that I might follow you to fullness of life. Beloved, I empty myself in you.

Ponder for the Day

What aspects of the coming year feel bleak right now? How can you prepare a way for Christ there?

Prayer for the Evening

Jesus, God's Love, you are always ready to meet us in prayer. Increase my longing to dwell with you in my quiet contemplation. Beloved, come to me.

To listen to "In the Bleak Midwinter," scan the QR code or visit

Sunday, January 11

Feast of the Baptism of the Lord

What can I give him, poor as I am? . . .
Yet what I can, I give him, give my heart.

As we've been contemplating Jesus's arrival among us to share life with us, we remember today that he submitted to baptism so that it would become a way for us to be claimed and marked forever as children of God. It is fitting to conclude this Christmas season by recalling the power of Baptism, which binds us to the divine life of Christ alive in the Church.

We who have encountered God's love this season have only one way to deepen our experience of the gift we've been given: to participate in it by sharing it with others. This love has changed us—it is good news that we are called to proclaim by the way we live. Our baptism emboldens us to keep busy building the kingdom of God as members of Christ's Body.

Prayer for the Morning

Spirit of Holiness, in our baptism, you give us the gifts we need to live fully into our identity as sons and daughters of God. Increase the virtues of faith, hope, and love in me that I might live with hope the Christian life. Spirit of Joy, I give you my heart.

Ponder for the Day

What spiritual gifts have you received this season? How will you try to carry them into the new year?

Prayer for the Evening

Spirit of Holiness, you revealed yourself to Christ at his baptism and come upon us in the Church's Baptism even now. Re-create me with the fire of your love, and help me share the gifts you give me for the life of the world. Spirit of Life, sustain me.

www.avemariapress.com/pages/away-in-a-manger-music.

COMPLETE LYRICS

FIRST WEEK OF ADVENT

SAVIOR OF THE NATIONS COME

Author: St. Ambrose | Translator: William M. Reynolds

Savior of the nations, come; virgin's son, make here thy home!
Marvel now, O heav'n and earth, that the Lord chose such a birth.
Not by human flesh and blood, but the Spirit of our God,
was the Word of God made flesh-woman's offspring, pure and fresh.

Wondrous birth! O wondrous Child of the virgin undefiled!
Tho' by all the world disowned, still to be in heav'n enthroned.

From the Father forth he came and returneth to the same,
captive leading death and hell-high the song of triumph swell

Thou, the Father's only Son, hast o'er sin the vict'ry won.
Boundless shall thy kingdom be; when shall we its glories see?

Brightly doth thy manger shine, glorious is its light divine.
Let not sin o'ercloud this light ever be our faith thus bright.

Praise to God the Father, sing, praise to God, the Son, our king,
praise to God the Spirit be ever and eternally.

KEEP YOUR LAMPS TRIMMED AND BURNING

African American Spiritual

Keep your lamps trimmed and burning,
keep your lamps trimmed and burning,
keep your lamps trimmed and burning,
the day is drawing nigh.

Refrain:
Children, don't get weary,
children, don't get weary,
children, don't get weary
till your work is done.

Darker midnight lies before us,
darker midnight lies before us,
darker midnight lies before us,
the day is drawing nigh. *Refrain*

For the morning soon is breaking,
for the morning soon is breaking,
for the morning soon is breaking,
the day is drawing nigh. *Refrain*

Christian journey soon be over,
Christian journey soon be over,
Christian journey soon be over,
the day is drawing nigh. *Refrain*

WATCHMAN, TELL US OF THE NIGHT
Author: John Bowring

Watchman, tell us of the night, what its signs of promise are.
Traveler, what a wondrous sight: see that glory-beaming star.
Watchman, does its beauteous ray news of joy or hope foretell?
Traveler, yes; it brings the day, promised day of Israel.

Watchman, tell us of the night; higher yet that star ascends.
Traveler, blessedness and light, peace and truth its course portends.
Watchman, will its beams alone gild the spot that gave them birth?
Traveler, ages are its own; see, it bursts o'er all the earth.

Watchman, tell us of the night, for the morning seems to dawn.
Traveler, shadows take their flight; doubt and terror are withdrawn.
Watchman, you may go your way; hasten to your quiet home.
Traveler, we rejoice today, for Emmanuel has come!

Second Week of Advent

Lo, How a Rose E'er Blooming

Traditional German | Translator: Theodore Baker

Lo, how a Rose e'er blooming
from tender stem hath sprung!
Of Jesse's lineage coming
as men of old have sung.
It came, a flower bright,
amid the cold of winter
when half-gone was the night.

Isaiah 'twas foretold it,
the Rose I have in mind:
with Mary we behold it,
the virgin mother kind.
To show God's love aright
she bore to men a Savior
when half-gone was the night.

This Flower, whose fragrance tender
with sweetness fills the air,
dispels with glorious splendor
the darkness everywhere.
True man, yet very God,
from sin and death he saves us
and lightens every load.

Mañanitas Guadalupanas

Traditional Spanish

Buenos días, paloma blanca,
hoy te vengo a saludar,
saludando a tu belleza
en tu trono celestial.

Good morning, White Dove,
today I come to greet you,
saluting your beauty
on your heavenly throne.

Eres madre del Creador
que a mi corazón encantas.

You are the mother of the Creator
who enchants my heart.

Gracias te doy con amor.
Buenos días, paloma blanca.

Niña linda, niña santa,
tu dulce nombre alabar
porque eres tan sacrosanta,
hoy te vengo a saludar.

Reluciente como el alba,
pura, sencilla y sin mancha;
qué gusto recibe mi alma.
Buenos días, paloma blanca.

Qué linda está la mañana,
el aroma de las flores.
Despiden suaves olores
antes de romper el alba.

Mi pecho con voz ufana,
gracias te doy, madre mía,
en este dichoso día
antes de romper el alba.

Cielo azul yo te convido
en este dichoso día
a que prestes tu hermosura
a las flores de María.

Madre mía de Guadalupe,
dame ya tu bendición.
Recibe estas mañanitas
de mi humilde corazón.

I give you thanks with love.
Good morning, White Dove.

Pretty maiden, holy maiden,
your sweet name to praise
because you are so sacred
today I come to greet you.

Radiant as the dawn,
pure, simple, and spotless;
what pleasure my soul receives.
Good morning, White Dove.

How beautiful is the morning,
the scent of the flowers.
They give off soft fragrance
before the dawn breaks.

My chest with a proud voice,
I give you thanks, my mother,
on this blessed day
before the dawn breaks.

Blue sky I invite you
on this happy day
to lend your beauty
to the flowers of Mary.

My Mother of Guadalupe,
give me now your blessing.
Receive these songs
from my humble heart.

On Jordan's Bank the Baptist's Cry

Author: Charles Coffin | Translator: John Chandler

On Jordan's bank the Baptist's cry announces that the Lord is nigh.
Awake and harken, for he brings glad tidings of the King of kings!

Then cleansed be every life from sin: make straight the way for God within,
and let us all our hearts prepare for Christ to come and enter there.

We hail you as our Savior, Lord, our refuge and our great reward.
Without your grace we waste away like flowers that wither and decay.

Stretch forth your hand, our health restore, and make us rise to fall no more.
O let your face upon us shine and fill the world with love divine.

All praise to you, eternal Son, whose advent has our freedom won,
whom with the Father we adore, and Holy Spirit, evermore.

Comfort, Comfort Ye My People

Author: Johann Olearius | Translator: Catherine Winkworth

Comfort, comfort ye my people,
speak ye peace, thus saith our God.
Comfort those who sit in darkness,
mourning neath their sorrows' load.
Speak ye to Jerusalem
of the peace that waits for them;
tell her that her sins I cover,
and her warfare now is over.

Yes, her sins our God will pardon,
blotting out each dark misdeed;
all that well deserved his anger
he will no more see nor heed.
She hath suffered many a day,
now her griefs have passed away;
God will change her pining sadness
into ever-springing gladness.

For the herald's voice is crying
in the desert far and near,
bidding all to true repentance,
since the kingdom now is here.
Oh, that warning cry obey,
now prepare for God a way;
Let the valleys rise to meet him,
and the hills bow down to greet him.

Make ye straight what long was crooked,
make the rougher places plain;
let your hearts be true and humble,
as befits his holy reign;
for the glory of the Lord
now o'er earth is shed abroad,
and all flesh shall see the token
that his Word is never broken.

WAKE, AWAKE, FOR NIGHT IS FLYING

Authors: Philipp Nicolai and Catherine Winkworth

Wake, awake, for night is flying,
the watchmen on the heights are crying;
awake, Jerusalem, at last.
Midnight hears the welcome voices,
and at the thrilling cry rejoices:
"Come forth, you maidens! Night is past.
The Bridegroom comes! Awake;
your lamps with gladness take!"
Alleluia!
Prepare yourselves to meet the Lord,
whose light has stirred the waiting guard.

Zion hears the watchmen singing,
and in her heart new joy is springing.
She wakes, she rises from her gloom,
for her Lord comes down all-glorious,
and strong in grace, in truth victorious.
Her star is ris'n; her light is come.

O, come, you Blessed One,
Lord Jesus, God's own Son.
Sing hosanna!
We go until the halls we view
where You have bid us dine with You.

Now let all the heav'ns adore You,
and saints and angels sing before You.
The harps and cymbals all unite.
Of one pearl each shining portal,
where, dwelling with the choir immortal,
we gather 'round Your dazzling light.
No eye has seen, no ear
has yet been trained to hear
what joy is ours!
Crescendos rise; Your halls resound;
hosannas blend in cosmic sound.

PEOPLE, LOOK EAST

Author: Eleanor Farjeon

People, look east. The time is near
of the crowning of the year.
Make your house fair as you are able,
trim the hearth and set the table.
People, look east and sing today:
Love, the guest, is on the way.

Furrows, be glad. Though earth is bare,
one more seed is planted there:
give up your strength the seed to nourish,
that in course the flower may flourish.
People, look east and sing today:
Love, the rose, is on the way.

Birds, though you long have ceased to build,
guard the nest that must be filled.
Even the hour when wings are frozen
God for fledging time has chosen.
People, look east and sing today:
Love, the bird, is on the way.

Stars, keep the watch. When night is dim
one more light the bowl shall brim,
shining beyond the frosty weather,
bright as sun and moon together.
People, look east and sing today:
Love, the star, is on the way.

Angels, announce with shouts of mirth
Christ who brings new life to earth.
Set every peak and valley humming
with the word, the Lord is coming.
People, look east and sing today:
Love, the Lord, is on the way.

THE ANGEL GABRIEL FROM HEAVEN CAME

Traditional Basque | Translator: S. Baring-Gould

The angel Gabriel from heaven came,
his wings as drifted snow, his eyes as flame;
"All hail," said he to meek and lowly Mary,
"most highly favored maiden." Gloria!

"I come from heav'n to tell the Lord's decree:
a blessed virgin mother you shall be.
Your son shall be Immanuel, by seers foretold,
most highly favored maiden." Gloria!

Then gentle Mary meekly bowed her head;
"To me be as it pleases God," she said.
"My soul shall laud and magnify his holy name."
Most highly favored maiden, Gloria!

Of her, Immanuel, the Christ, was born
in Bethlehem, all on a Christmas morn,
and Christian folk throughout the world will ever say,
"Most highly favored maiden." Gloria!

Angels We Have Heard on High

Traditional French

Angels we have heard on high,
sweetly singing o'er the plains;
and the mountains in reply
echoing their joyous strains.

Refrain:
Gloria in excelsis Deo!
Gloria in excelsis Deo!

Shepherds, why this jubilee?
Why your joyous strains prolong?
What the gladsome tidings be
which inspire your heav'nly song? *Refrain*

Come to Bethlehem and see
him whose birth the angels sing.
Come, adore on bended knee
Christ the Lord, the newborn King. *Refrain*

See him in a manger laid,
whom the choirs of angels praise.
Mary, Joseph, lend your aid
while our hearts in love we raise. *Refrain*

Away in a Manger

Attributed to Martin Luther

Away in a manger, no crib for a bed,
the little Lord Jesus laid down his sweet head;
the stars in the heavens looked down where he lay,
the little Lord Jesus asleep on the hay.

The cattle are lowing, the Baby awakes,
but little Lord Jesus, no crying he makes.

I love thee, Lord Jesus, look down from the sky
and stay by my side until morning is nigh.

Be near me, Lord Jesus; I ask thee to stay
close by me forever, and love me, I pray.
Bless all the dear children in thy tender care,
and fit us for heaven, to live with thee there.

The Magnificat

Luke 1:46–55

And Mary said:
"My soul proclaims the greatness of the Lord;
my spirit rejoices in God my savior.
For he has looked upon his handmaid's lowliness;
behold, from now on will all ages call me blessed.
The Mighty One has done great things for me,
and holy is his name.
His mercy is from age to age
to those who fear him.
He has shown might with his arm,
dispersed the arrogant of mind and heart.
He has thrown down the rulers from their thrones
but lifted up the lowly.
The hungry he has filled with good things;
the rich he has sent away empty.
He has helped Israel his servant,
remembering his mercy,
according to his promise to our fathers,
to Abraham and to his descendants forever."

Let All Mortal Flesh Keep Silence

Translator: Gerard Moultrie

Let all mortal flesh keep silence,
and with fear and trembling stand;
ponder nothing earthly minded,
for, with blessing in his hand,

Christ our God to earth descendeth,
our full homage to demand.

King of kings, yet born of Mary,
as of old on earth he stood,
Lord of lords, in human vesture,
in the body and the blood.
He will give to all the faithful
his own self for heav'nly food.

Rank on rank the host of heaven
spreads its vanguard on the way,
as the Light of light descendeth
from the realms of endless day,
that the pow'rs of hell may vanish
as the darkness clears away.

At his feet the six-winged seraph,
cherubim with sleepless eye,
veil their faces to the Presence,
as with ceaseless voice they cry,
"Alleluia, alleluia,
alleluia, Lord Most High!"

O LITTLE TOWN OF BETHLEHEM

Author: Phillips Brooks

O little town of Bethlehem,
how still we see thee lie!
Above thy deep and dreamless sleep
the silent stars go by.
Yet in thy dark streets shineth
the everlasting light;
the hopes and fears of all the years
are met in thee tonight.

For Christ is born of Mary;
and, gathered all above,
while mortals sleep, the angels keep
their watch of wond'ring love.

O morning stars, together
proclaim the holy birth,
and praises sing to God the King,
and peace to men on earth.

How silently, how silently,
the wondrous gift is giv'n!
So God imparts to human hearts
the blessings of his heav'n.
No ear may hear his coming,
but in this world of sin,
where meek souls will receive him still,
the dear Christ enters in.

O holy Child of Bethlehem,
descend to us, we pray;
cast out our sin and enter in;
be born in us today.
We hear the Christmas angels,
the great glad tidings tell;
O come to us, abide with us,
our Lord Emmanuel!

It Came Upon the Midnight Clear

Author: Edmund H. Sears

It came upon the midnight clear,
that glorious song of old,
from angels bending near the earth
to touch their harps of gold:
"Peace on the earth, good will to all,
from heaven's all-gracious King."
The world in solemn stillness lay,
to hear the angels sing.

Still through the cloven skies they come
with peaceful wings unfurled,
and still their heavenly music floats
o'er all the weary world;

above its sad and lowly plains,
they bend on hovering wing,
and ever o'er its Babel sounds
the blessed angels sing.

And ye, beneath life's crushing load,
whose forms are bending low,
who toil along the climbing way
with painful steps and slow,
look now! for glad and golden hours
come swiftly on the wing.
O rest beside the weary road,
and hear the angels sing!

For lo! the days are hastening on,
by prophet seen of old,
when with the ever-circling years
shall come the time foretold
when peace shall over all the earth
its ancient splendors fling,
and the whole world send back the song
which now the angels sing.

In the Bleak Midwinter

Author: Christina Georgina Rossetti

In the bleak midwinter frosty wind made moan,
earth stood hard as iron, water like a stone:
snow had fallen, snow on snow, snow on snow,
in the bleak midwinter, long ago.

Our God, heaven cannot hold him, nor earth sustain;
heaven and earth shall flee away when he comes to reign:
in the bleak midwinter a stable place sufficed
the Lord God Almighty, Jesus Christ.

Enough for him whom cherubim worship night and day,
a breastful of milk and a mangerful of hay:
enough for him whom angels fall down before,
the ox and ass and camel which adore.

Angels and archangels may have gathered there,
cherubim and seraphim thronged the air,
but only his mother, in her maiden bliss,
worshiped the Beloved with a kiss.

What can I give him, poor as I am?
If I were a shepherd, I would bring a lamb,
if I were a wise man, I would do my part,
yet what I can, I give him, give my heart.

Founded in 1865 by Fr. Edward Sorin, CSC, **Ave Maria Press** is an apostolate of the Congregation of Holy Cross, United States Province of Priests and Brothers. Ave is a nonprofit Catholic publishing ministry that serves the spiritual and formative needs of the Church and its schools, institutions, and ministers; Christian individuals and families; and others seeking spiritual nourishment.

Ave remains one of the oldest continually operating Catholic publishing houses in the country and a leader in publishing Catholic high school religion textbooks, ministry resources, and books on prayer and spirituality.

In the tradition of Holy Cross, Ave is committed, as an educator in the faith, to help people know, love, and serve God and to spread the gospel of Jesus Christ through books and other resources.

Ave Maria Press perpetuates Fr. Sorin's vision to honor Mary and provide an important outlet for good Catholic writing.

Josh Noem is the editorial director at Ave Maria Press. He began his writing career as a Catholic journalist and served as editor of the FaithND and Grotto Network platforms before joining Ave in 2022. His book, *The End of Ending*, was recognized as one of the best Catholic novels of 2021.

Noem grew up in the Black Hills of South Dakota and earned a master of divinity degree from the University of Notre Dame.

Noem and his family live in South Bend, Indiana. Find more of his writing at joshnoem.substack.com.

Website: joshnoem.substack.com
Instagram: @josh.noem

DID YOU ENJOY THIS ADVENT DEVOTIONAL?

Continue Your Musical Journey Throughout Lent

with *WHAT*
Wonderous LOVE

DAILY PRAYERS

FOR *Lent* AND *Holy Week 2026*

Rooted in the lyrics of beloved hymns, this daily companion invites you to pray, reflect, and even hum along to powerful songs of the season, including:

- "Blessed Assurance"
- "I Know That My Redeemer Lives"
- "Down by the Riverside"
- "What Wondrous Love Is This"

Find a full playlist to listen to throughout the season!

Listen to all of the carols and hymns from this book in one place by scanning the code, or visit **avemariapress.com/what-wonderous-love-music**.

Find this title wherever books and eBooks are sold.